Ladybird Readers

Racing with Scuderia Ferrari
Activity Book

Written by Catrin Morris

Song lyrics on page 16 written by David Smith

 Singing *  Reading  Speaking   Critical thinking

 Spelling   Writing   Listening *

* To complete these activities, listen to tracks 2, 3, and 4 of the audio download available at www.ladybirdeducation.co.uk

1 Work with a friend. Look at the pictures.
Ask and answer *What is this?* or *What are these?*
questions, and use *This is* or *These are.*

1

What is this?

This is a trophy.

2

3

4

5

2 Look and read. Write the correct words on the lines. 📖 ✏️

| gas | flag | lap | pit stop | trophy | tires |

1 some ......**gas**......

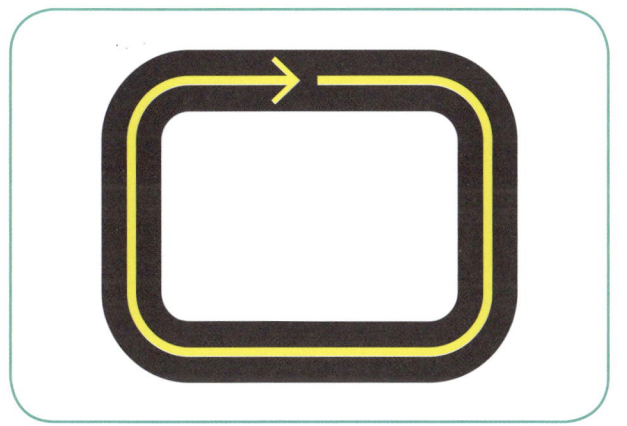

2 a ....

3 a ....

4 a ....

5 some ....

6 a ....

Look, match and write the words.

1
race — am

2
over — phy

3
pit st — re

4
te — op

5
tro — take

6
ti — track

1 __racetrack__   2 _____

3 _____   4 _____

5 _____   6 _____

4

4 Listen and complete the sentences.
Where are these things or people? 🎧*

1 Felipe Massa

He's on the

...... racetrack ....

2 Ferrari team

It's in the

....

3 winner

He's driving under the

....

4 trophy

It's in his

....

5 tires

They are going on the

....

6 Ferrari

They're in front of the

other ....

Look and read. Choose the correct words and write them on the lines. 📖 ✏️

overtake

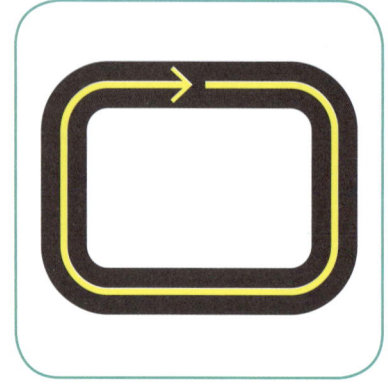

lap

flag

pit stop

trophy

team

1 Racing drivers always try to .... *overtake* ....

2 When a driver needs new tires, he uses a ....

3 Before the race, there is a practice ....

4 The winner is the first to drive under the ....

5 There are a lot of people in the Ferrari ....

6 The winner of a Grand Prix gets a ....

6 Read and circle the correct verbs.

1  A Grand Prix race (is) / **are** usually 190 miles long, and it **take** / **takes** about two hours to drive.

2  A lot of work **happen** / **happens** before a Grand Prix.

3  When the drivers and engineers **arrive,** / **arrives,** they **go** / **goes** to look at the racetrack.

4  On the Friday before the race, each team **have** / **has** two lots of practice time before the first qualifying lap.

7 **Look at the pictures and read the questions. Write complete sentences.**

1

What is the practice time used for?

It is used to get information.

2

Why must the driver be careful in qualifying?

....

....

....

3

Why do all the drivers want to start first?

....

....

....

4

What is it important to do in the qualifying lap?

....

....

8 Write *What*, *Which*, or *How*.

1 ....What.... can help decide the winner of a race?

2 .... much gas the team puts in the car.

3 .... tires they choose.

4 .... quickly the race starts.

5 .... fast the car goes through the pit stops.

Pit stops

Cars still use pit stops for other things, like changing tires. There are usually one to three stops in a race.

The car must stop, change tires, and start again, in two or three seconds.

Changing tires at a pit stop.

36   37

1 Cars come fast into a pit stop. ✓

2 How fast the car goes through the pit stops isn't important.

3 The team helps the drivers at pit stops.

4 There are usually ten pit stops in a race.

5 The car must stop, change tires, and start again, in two or three seconds.

10 Listen and order the text. Write 1—6. *

.... The driver gets champagne.

.... The driver gets the race trophy.

.... The driver throws champagne on the team and the other drivers.

.... The driver waves to the people watching.

1 The first driver to drive under the flag is the winner.

.... The car drives another lap.

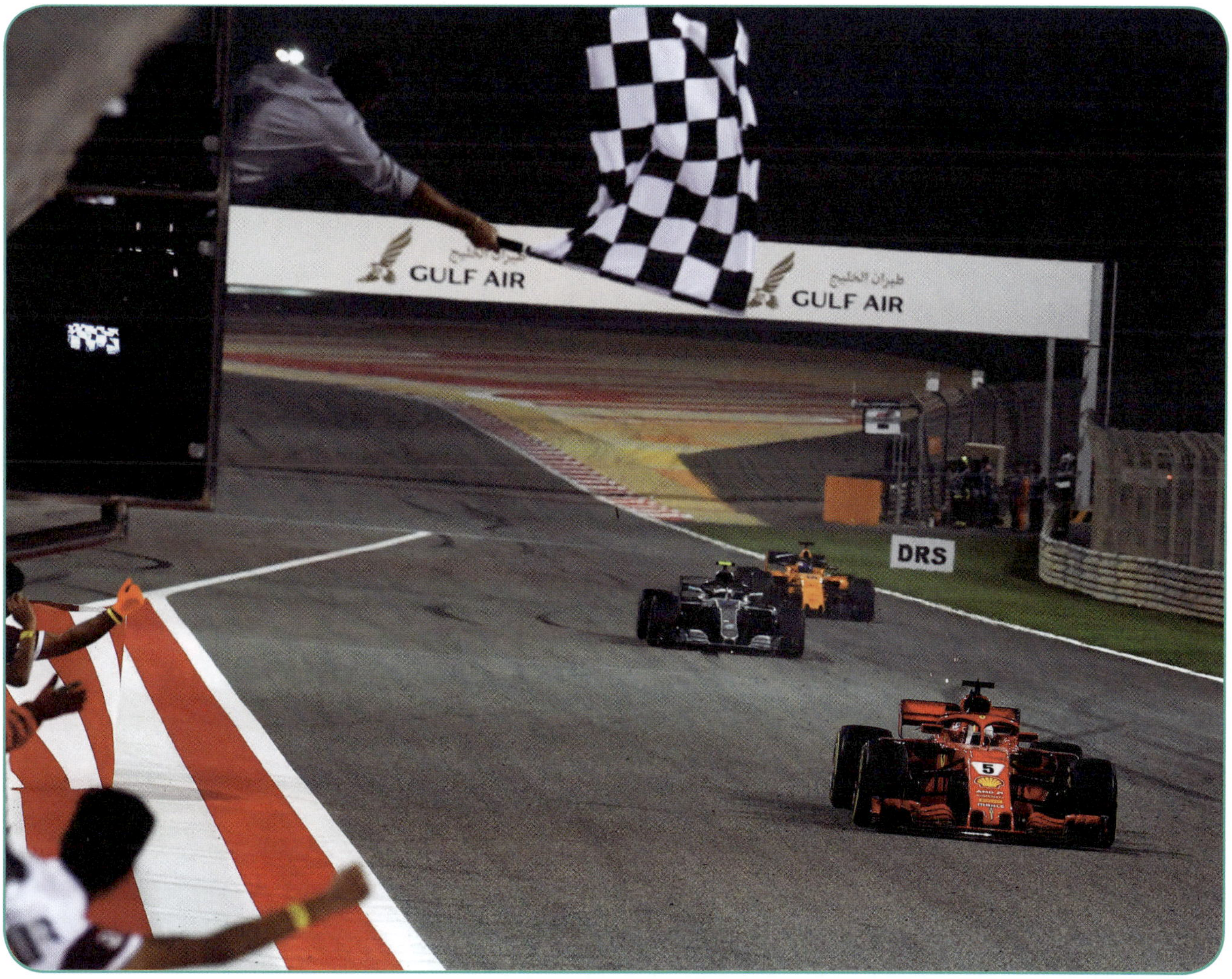

* To complete this activity, listen to track 3 of the audio download available at **www.ladybirdeducation.co.uk**

11 Look at the pictures.
Put a ✓ in the correct boxes.

1

a gas ✓

b gaz ☐

2

a tim ☐

b team ☐

3

a flag ☐

b fleg ☐

4

a lap ☐

b leap ☐

5

a laits ☐

b lights ☐

6

a winer ☐

b winner ☐

12 Find the words. 📖

```
f  l  a  g  f  s  l  p  r  n
g  q  l  p  t  e  a  m  a  b
p  i  t  s  t  o  p  d  c  s
u  d  i  h  r  v  n  x  e  p
r  j  r  c  o  e  i  k  t  d
g  s  e  u  p  r  m  w  r  e
a  l  i  g  h  t  s  h  a  r
s  h  m  v  y  a  v  b  c  e
o  g  z  b  j  k  q  h  k  s
n  w  y  u  n  e  g  z  b  h
```

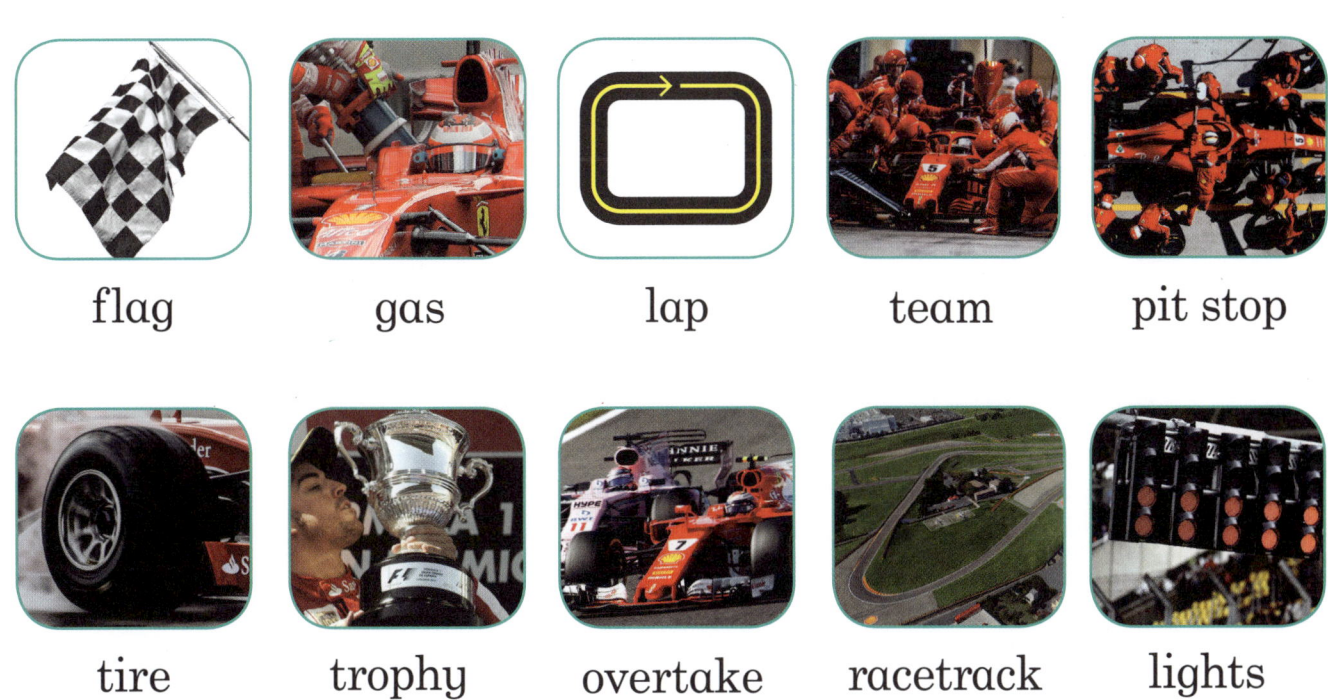

flag   gas   lap   team   pit stop

tire   trophy   overtake   racetrack   lights

13 Work with a friend. Help the Ferrari racing driver win the Grand Prix. Use the words in the box.

go straight   turn right   go to the end

turn left   stop at the pit stop   overtake

go under the flag

Go straight.
Then turn right . . .

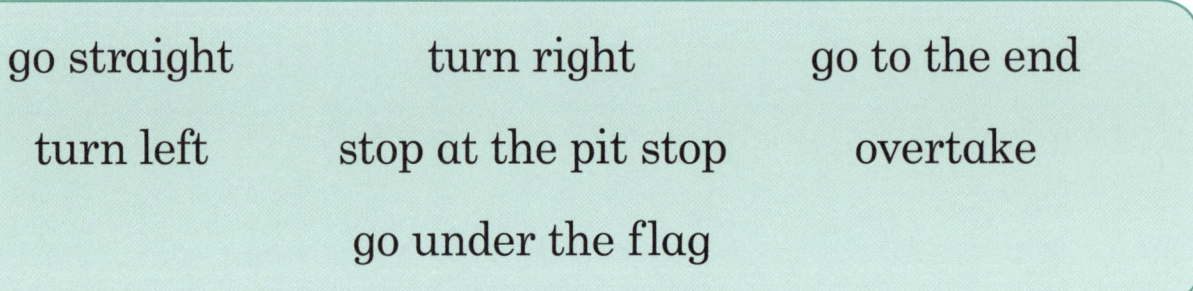

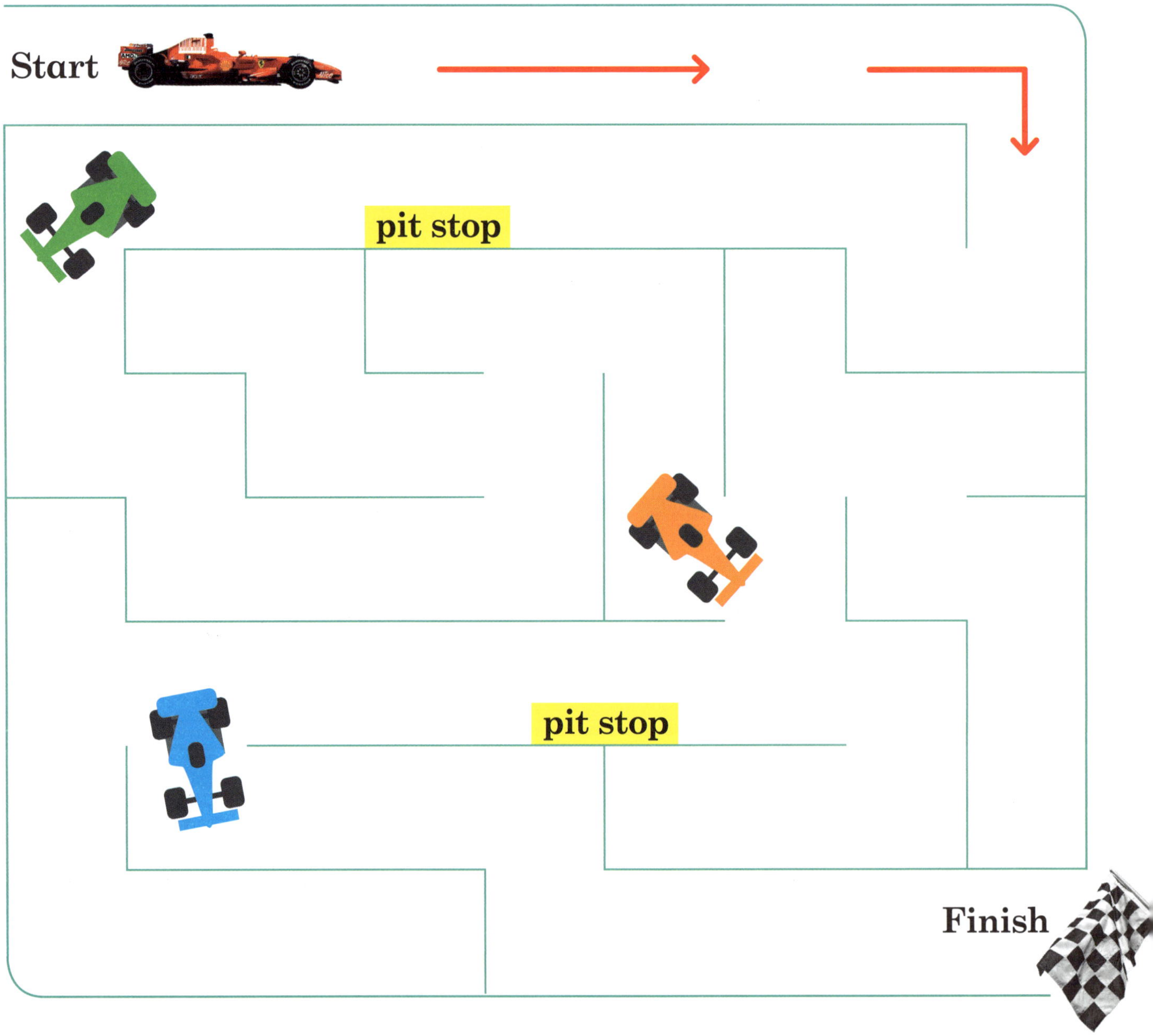

Start

pit stop

pit stop

Finish

14

14 Read and circle the correct words.

1 Teams do these things before a race.

(look at information) (practice time) stop at a pit stop (work on the car)

2 Racing drivers do these things in a race.

drive around corners get a trophy look at information stop at a pitstop

3 At the pit stop, drivers can get . . .

a trophy. champagne. a flag. tires.

4 At the end of the race, there are these things.

a flag practice time champagne a trophy

Grand Prix, it's the Grand Prix.
Racing with Ferrari!

A lot of work happens before a Grand Prix.
The qualifying laps decide each driver's starting place,
In Monaco, at the Hungaroring, or in Abu Dhabi.
Sunday is the day of the big, big race.

Grand Prix, it's the Grand Prix.
Racing with Ferrari!

Ferrari brings its team to the racetrack,
All the drivers study it very, very carefully.
Will they feel like winners when they come back?
Does the car need more gas, or is it too heavy?

Grand Prix, it's the Grand Prix.
Racing with Ferrari!

The cars change tires at a pit stop.
Stop, change, start again—one, two, three.
First one under the flag is the winner,
The happy driver gets the race trophy.

Grand Prix, it's the Grand Prix.
Racing with Ferrari!
Grand Prix, it's the Grand Prix.
Racing with Ferrari!

 * To complete this activity, listen to track 4 of the audio download available at www.ladybirdeducation.co.uk